MY PRAYERBOOK
For Prevailing In Prayer

By
Anthony Obasola Shoderu
B.Sc., FCA.ACS.
obashoderu@gmail.com

TABLE OF CONTENT

DEDICATION

The adaptation of the books of The Holy Bible resulting in "MY PRAYERBOOK- For Prevailing In Prayer" is another of my humble contributions to Christian Literature. This time it is in the areas of Personal Devotion and Prayer through Scriptures.

It is dedicated first to the Holy Spirit who, among His many other functions, inspires and enlightens believers and is ever praying, for them, in words that cannot be described, **Romans 8: 36b**. It is also dedicated to those whom the Holy Spirit has inspired and led into the Intercession Ministry.

ACKNOWLEDGMENTS

The works and contributions of the following organizations and individuals are sincerely acknowledged with gratitude: the King George Version of the Holy Bible, Dake's Annotated Reference Bible, by Finis Jennings Dake; New Bible Dictionary (Second Edition) by Inter-Varsity Press, Leicester, England; my wife, Tola and other members of my family.

INTRODUCTION

God is enthralled when man is drawn close to Him in prayer. Man's attitude to 'meditate day and night' (**Psalm 1: 2**) on God's word is most pleasing to God. Perhaps in the realization of God's love for a better relationship with man, Apostle Paul counsels believers to pray without ceasing, (**1 Thessalonians 5: 17**). James on his part admonishes believers to pray in affliction and sing the Psalms when joyful (**James 5: 13**). Graciously, there are Psalms to suit all occasions, situations, and circumstances!

'Watch and pray, that ye enter not into temptation', (**Matthew 26: 41**), is the counsel from the Messiah, our Lord Jesus Christ himself to believers. Happily enough, there are Psalms to suit all purposes, occasions, situations, and circumstances!

Singing and praying the Psalms is one of the ways through which believers pray without ceasing. The Book of Psalms is the 19th Book of the Holy Bible and is found in the section known as the Old Testament. Quotations and references are made to the Psalms in many Books of the Bible in both the Old Testament and New Testament. It is important to appreciate that the Book of Psalms has many chapters containing all forms of prayer. Other Books of the Bible, like Isaiah, Jeremiah, Ezekiel, and others have their shares of different types of prayers.

This Prayer is now personally yours. Henceforth, you should call it, MY PRAYERBOOK. Calling it MY PRAYERBOOK is your very first step of Personalization.

CHAPTER 1

Effective Use of MY PRAYERBOOK

Prayer is a priceless privilege for all believers. Their many and varied devotional and supplication uses to make them worth more than a jewel, even jewels of inestimable price. Whether praying in tongues, chanting or dancing them, or praying them in silently heartfelt meditation or supplication, Praying remains jewels of inestimable spiritual, emotional, and physical value to all God's children.

Deriving utmost benefits from your use of MY PRAYER-BOOK requires proper knowledge and understanding of how it is to be used.

As weapons of multidimensional usages such as in praise and worship, warfare prayer, supplication or intercessory; as ornaments to be worn for and on different occasions; as light and lamp to illuminate your path thus banishing the darkness of various shades, intensities, and thickness, etc.; Prayer must therefore be approached with good knowledge and clear understanding for effective and result-oriented usage.

Some warfare Prayers, such as **Psalms 7, 35, and 68** to mention just a few, require that you, the supplicant be free and guiltless of what you are complaining of and demanding justice and vindication over from our ever just and incomparably righteous God Almighty.

Whereas **Psalm 1** is very potent in the hands of a righteous believer to pray for all-round prosperity; yet, it is not at all favorable in the hand of anyone who still lives in sin and cherishes it. In fact, this is very dangerous for sinners in that unless they repent it is utter condemnation for them, thus:

For the LORD knoweth the way of the righteous: but the way of the ungodly shall perish.
Psalm 1: 6

Whereas the above warning may seem relevant in particular to supplication, this is not so. Coming to worship God requires cleanliness of hand and mind, as only those with such are allowed in His presence.

Who shall ascend into the hill of the LORD? Or who shall stand in his holy place? He that hath clean hands, and a pure heart; who hath not lifted up his soul unto vanity, nor sworn deceitfully. He shall receive the blessing from the LORD, and righteousness from the God of his salvation.
Psalm 24: 3 - 5

God abhors the offering of a sinner whereas that of the righteous is a delight to Him.

The sacrifice of the wicked is an abomination to the LORD: but the prayer of the upright is his delight.
Proverbs 15: 8

Bearing in mind that worship is also an offering, supposedly one of a sweet savor to satisfy Almighty God's pleasure! The Scripture says the offering of a sinner is an abomination.

The one offering the worship, the vessel bearing the worship must be separated from the contaminant. Sin is a contaminant! Here, in the place of worship of the Most High is separation from sin that is sanctification, is most required

The point being made and stressed here is that knowledge and clear understanding are required. The believer who desires to profit from the use of Psalms requires them absolutely. Remember the word of God concerning the absolute necessity to acquire and not to reject knowledge.

My people are destroyed for lack of knowledge: because thou hast rejected knowledge, I will also reject thee.
Hosea 4: 6

To derive maximum benefit in the use of this PRAYERBOOK, the believer is called to a life of purity, without which no man can stand in the presence of our holy and righteous, though merciful God, let alone see Him.

Entering the Throne of Mercy
It is heart-warming that his love enables us to approach His Throne of Mercy, to which He has graciously invited us to come boldly unto, **Hebrews 4: 16**. Bearing in mind that He has endowed us with His righteousness, **Isaiah 54: 17b**, it befits believers to appreciate His holiness and blemish-less requirement by purifying themselves.

What this simply entails is, as a believer desiring to profit greatly in the use of MY PRAYERBOOK, you need to be conscious of your need to be in a state of purity before and as you enter into God's presence. In this state of purity of body, soul, and spirit your devotion, worship or supplication will be accepted, as a sweet-smelling oblation by the Almighty God, through Christ Jesus.

Among the many ways of doing the above is to always earnestly pray for forgiveness. Praying for forgiveness should normally come from the heart of the believer with deep regret and sorrow for sins committed and, desire to forsake them. The believer must surrender self to the Holy Spirit for cleansing and leading, **Romans 8: 14.** In this state the believer is led to realize that:

He that covereth his sins shall not prosper: but whoso confesseth and forsaketh them shall have mercy.
Proverbs 28:13

You, as a believer, must then proceed to deal with your sin and be right with God, who is ever merciful.

And if any man sin, we have an advocate with the Father, Jesus Christ the righteous. And he is the propitiation for our sins: and not for ours only, but also for the sins of the whole world. *1 John 2: 1b – 2.*

Keys to the Use of MY PRAYERBOOK

The following are essential keys to the effective and prevailing use of Psalms: are Meditation, Mental-Visualization, Vocalization, Personalization, and Memorization.

Meditation

You require concentration and deep thought on the purpose, goals, and objective in focus as well as the chosen Bible passages. Passages chosen must bear very close resemblance if not identical to the issues, matters, or complaints you are about to table before the Throne of Grace. This is the reason you need a quiet and conducive environment, devoid of distraction when embarking on using this Prayer-Book.

Visualization

This is mental and spiritual development. You attain it through your deep concentration on the subject matter of your prayer. Soon, the Holy Spirit will help you to form an image or images as the case may be, in your mind. These are mental images that you can then see in your mind's eyes. You can see the challenges which are eventually dissolved, that is they disappear, resulting in victory for you.

Vocalization

Here, you are to speak, chant, or sing the relevant chosen Scriptures, Hymns, or Psalms to address the issues, matters, or challenges that you have brought to the Throne of Grace. This is very much in nature of using this Prayer book. If you are using Scriptures, Hymns Psalms, or chant them, vocalizing the Scriptures or Hymns helps increase your concentration, meditation, and visualization.

Personalization

Here is your practical way of giving life to your worship of Jehovah or in supplication to Him. This can be, you Jane, bringing your offering - worship to Jehovah. So also it can be you, John, asking the Almighty God for direction as to which of two job-offers to accept or future partner to choose. It could be you, Christie, interceding, praying for God to heal Sophia, your new Christian Fellowship member.

Memorization
This emphasizes your need to commit your favorite Bible passages and other Scriptures to memory. This is necessary as some occasions may not permit you to bring out your Prayer-Book to pray from.

CHAPTER 2

Praise And Worship As 'The Weapon'

The Scripture Stresses and encourages the goodness of offering thanks and praises to God who delights to hear our prayer, **Psalm 65: 2**, and that He resides inside His peoples' praises.

It is a good thing to give thanks unto the LORD, and to sing praises unto Thy name, O most High.
Psalm 92: 1

Whereas believers offer prayers to God need to rise and ascend to Him, it is different when the believers praise and worship Him. The beauty of such prayer of worship and praises is that The Almighty comes in His glory with His angels and He resides in such prayer. Hear what the Psalmist says.

But Thou art holy, O Thou that inhabitests the praises of Israel.
Psalm 22: 3

Judah under Jehoshaphat as their King praised their way into victory over three mighty nations of the children of Moab, Ammon, and of mount Seir.

22. And when they began to sing and to praise, the LORD set ambushments against the children of Ammon, Moab, and mount Seir, which were come against Judah; and they were smitten. 23. For the children of Ammon and Moab stood up against the inhabitants of mount Seir, utterly to slay and destroy them: and when they had made an end of the inhabitants of Seir, everyone helped to destroy another.
2 Chronicles 20: 22 - 23

Added to the victory was the spoil of war in which victory was won for them by God. Judah did not lift a finger in their victory; God won the war and gave them victory.

And when Jehoshaphat and his people came to take away the spoil of them, they found among them in abundance both riches with the dead bodies, and precious jewels, which they stripped off for themselves, more than they could carry away: and they were three days in the gathering of the spoil, it was so much.*2 Chronicles 20: 25*

More encouraging is that believers' prayer never gets unnoticed or wasted. Senior heavenly beings, who worship daily in the presence of the Almighty God, have responsibility for the safe storage of their prayers.

The four beasts and four and twenty elders fell down before the Lamb, having every one of them harps, and golden vials full of odors, which are the prayers of saints.
Revelation 5: 8

Oh, Thou that hearest prayer, unto Thee shall all flesh com
Psalm65: 2

What else is there to wait for? Get down to prayer of Praise and Worship of the Almighty God and our Lord Jesus Christ.

BIBLE PASSAGE
PSALM 92: 1 – 2 & 4
1. IT IS A GOOD THING TO GIVE THANKS UNTO THE LORD, AND TO SING PRAISES UNTO THY NAME, O MOST HIGH: 2. To shew forth thy loving kindness in the morning, and thy faithfulness every night, 4. For thou, LORD, hast made me glad through thy work: I will triumph in the works of thy hands.

PRAYER
It is a joyful and pleasant time to spend in your presence O LORD to give praises and thanks to your Majesty.
Dear Lord and Heavenly Father you are worthy to be praised and worshipped for your great love towards me and all mankind.
I give you thanks and praises for your loving-kindness.
Eternal and unchanging and immutable God, I adore and worship your Excellency.
Holy and Mighty God, please accept my thanks, adoration, and worship, which I offer your Majesty in the name of Jesus Christ.
Amen.

BIBLE PASSAGE

PSALM 100: 1 - 5

1. Make a joyful noise unto the LORD, all ye lands. 2. Serve the LORD with gladness: come before his presence with singing. 3. Know ye that the LORD he is God: it is he that hath made us, and not we ourselves; we are his people, and the sheep of his pasture. 4. Enter into His gates with Thanksgiving, and into His courts with praise: be thankful unto Him, and bless His name. 5. For the LORD is good; his mercy is everlasting; and his truth endureth to all generations.

PRAYER

Dear heavenly Father, our LORD, God, and maker, it's with joy that I come into your presence.

O Almighty Father, I humble myself before your Majesty.

I worship at your foot-stool, even as I give you all the adoration, glory, and praises, in the name of my Lord and Savior Jesus Christ.

Father, LORD accept my worship, my adoration, praises, and thanks all of which I offer you in the name of Jesus Christ my Lord and Savior.

Amen.

BIBLE PASSAGE
PSALM 34: 1 - 4
1. I will bless the LORD at all times: his praise shall continually be in my mouth.2 My soul shall make her boast in the LORD: the humble shall hear thereof, and be glad. 3. O magnify the LORD with me, and let us exalt his name together. 4. I sought the LORD, and he heard me, and delivered me from all my fears.

PRAYER
My Dear Heavenly Father, You are the Father of all mercies,
I extol and bless Thee LORD for your mercy and kindness to me and all who are dear to me.
I magnify and exalt your holy name for the gift of a new day you've blessed me again with.
Be thou exalted eternally Oh Lord.
I return all the glory and adoration unto you, King of glory.
I pray you mercifully accept my adoration, praises, and worship of your Holiness in the name of Jesus Christ, my Lord.
Amen.

BIBLE PASSAGE
PSALM 65: 1 - 2 & 4

1. Praise waiteth for Thee, O God in Sion and unto Thee shall the vow be performed. 2. O Thou that hearest prayer. 4. Blessed is the man whom thou choosest, and causest to approach unto Thee, that he may dwell in thy courts: we shall be satisfied with the goodness of thy house, even of thy holy temple.

PRAYER
Almighty and eternal God,
You're worthy to be praised, honored, and adored
I come humbly to you in the name of my Lord and Saviour.
Father, Almighty, I worship and adore you.
I praise and thank you.
Please accept my worship and adoration.
Thank your Father
I prayed in Jesus' name.
Amen.

BIBLE PASSAGE
PSALM 30: 1 - 4

1. I will extol thee, O LORD; for thou hast lifted me up, and hast not made my foes to rejoice over me. 2. O LORD my God, I cried unto thee, and thou hast healed me. 3. O LORD, thou hast brought up my soul from the grave: thou hast kept me alive, that I should not go down to the pit.4. Sing unto the LORD, O ye saints of his, and give thanks at the remembrance of his holiness.

PRAYER
My Dear Heavenly Father, You are the Father of all mercies,

I extol you for your kindness and goodness to me and all who are dear to me.

It's a new day you've blessed me again with, be thou exalted Oh Lord.

I return all glory unto you, King of glory.

Be eternally exalted in my life O LORD my God.

Amen.

BIBLE PASSAGE

PSALM 136: 1 - 4 & 25

**1. O give thanks unto the LORD; for he is good:
for his mercy endureth forever. 2. O give thanks
unto the God of gods: for his mercy endureth
forever. 3. O give thanks to the Lord of lords: for
his mercy endureth forever. 4.To him who alone
doeth great wonders: for his mercy endureth
forever. 25. Who giveth food to all flesh: for his
mercy endureth forever.**

PRAYER

Almighty God and King of glory, I appreciate your
love, mercy, and kindness which endure forever.
I give you thanks and praises for your goodness and
loving-kindness upon me, my family, and my friends.
I thank your Majesty for your constant provisions
materially and spiritually.
I thank you for ensuring my security and defense
both physically and spiritually.
The great mighty and holy God, please accept my
thanks, praises, adoration, and worship which I offer
humbly in the name of Jesus Christ our Lord.
Amen.

CHAPTER 3

Praise and Worship With
Bible Personalities

The Scripture says man began to call upon the name of God, thus we find Noah praising and worshipping God after the Flood and his Ark beached on upon the mountains of Ararat, **Genesis 8: 4**. Noah followed with praise and worship of the Almighty God.

And Noah builded an altar unto the LORD; and took of every clean beast, and of every clean fowl, and offered burnt offerings on the altar.
Genesis 8: 20

God was pleased with Noah's offering and declared the following:

21 And the LORD smelled a sweet savor; and the LORD said in his heart, I will not again curse the ground any more for man's sake; for

the imagination of man's heart is evil from his youth; neither will I again smite any more everything living, as I have done. 22 While the earth remaineth, seedtime and harvest, and cold and heat, and summer and winter, and day and night shall not cease.
Genesis 8: 21 - 22

Thenceforth, men and women began to bless, praise, worship, and make supplications to God.

Aside from Noah mentioned above, other Scripture personalities who had an intimate relationship with God, ever praying to Him, were Moses, Joshua, Deborah, Eli, Samuel, David, Job, Isaiah, Jeremiah, Ezekiel, Daniel, and other prophets of the Old testament.

Among the Apostles and Prophets in the New Testament, who communed regularly with the Almighty God through Jesus Christ were Apostles Peter, John, Phillip, Agabus, Paul, and Barnabas.

BIBLE PASSAGE
LUKE 1: 46 - 47 & 49 - 50

46. And Mary said, My soul doth magnify the Lord, 47. And my spirit hath rejoiced in God my Saviour. 49. For he that is mighty hath done to me great things; and holy is his name. 50. And his mercy is on them that fear him from generation to generation.

PRAYER

O LORD our God, you are most worthy to be honored, praised, adored, and worshipped.

Dear LORD and my God, I praise your Holiness for your goodness to me and all that is mine.

LORD God of might and power I adore and worship your Majesty.

My dear Heavenly Father and Lord, in mercy, please accept my praises, adoration, and worship of your Excellency.

I thank you for the privilege of coming into your presence to praise, adore and worship your divine Majesty.

Thank you, LORD, for I prayed in Jesus' name.
Amen.

BIBLE PASSAGE
EXODUS 15: 2, 3, 9- 11

2. The **LORD** is my strength and song, and he is become my salvation: he is my God, and I will prepare him an habitation; my father's God, and I will exalt him. 3. The **LORD** is a man of war: the **LORD** is his name. 9. The enemy said, I will pursue, I will overtake, I will divide the spoil; my lust shall be satisfied upon them; I will draw my sword, my hand shall destroy them. 10. Thou didst blow with thy wind, the sea covered them: they sank as lead in the mighty waters. 11. Who is like unto thee, **O LORD**, among the gods? Who is like thee, glorious in holiness, fearful in praises, doing wonders?

PRAYER
O LORD my God, you are my strength and song and have become my salvation.

In mercy, you will favor and give me victory even as you did Israel over Egypt their oppressor.

O LORD I acknowledge your greatness for there is no one like you; you are glorious in holiness, fearful in praises, and forever doing wonders

Unto You, merciful and great LORD I return all glory, honor, and praises.

Accept them O LORD for Christ's sake, Amen

BIBLE PASSAGE
1 SAMUEL 2: 1, 2 & 10

1. My heart rejoiceth in the LORD, mine horn is exalted in the LORD: my mouth is enlarged over mine enemies; because I rejoice in thy salvation. 2. There is none holy as the LORD: for there is none beside thee: neither is there any rock like our God. 10. The adversaries of the LORD shall be broken to pieces; out of heaven shall he thunder upon them: the LORD shall judge the ends of the earth, and he shall give strength unto his king, and exalt the horn of his anointed

PRAYER
Our heavenly Father, I come humbly into your presence in the name of my Lord and Savior Jesus Christ

I humbly pray Your Excellency to remember me as you remembered Hannah of old.

Give me success and prosper me in my (business/ studies/ marriage/ work/ career/ endeavors.

Enlarge my mouth with joyful praises to you as you did Hannah.

Give me victory over all adversaries, dear LORD I pray in Jesus' hallowed name.

Amen.

BIBLE PASSAGE

ZEPHANIAH 17 - 19

17. The LORD thy God in the midst of thee is mighty; he will save, he will rejoice over thee with joy; he will rest in his love, he will joy over thee with singing. 18. I will gather them that are sorrowful for the solemn assembly, who are of thee, to whom the reproach of it was a burden. 19. Behold, at that time I will undo all that afflict thee: and I will save her that halteth, and gather her that was driven out; and I will get them praise and fame in every land where they have been put to shame.

PRAYER

Merciful Father, I'm greatly joyful knowing that Your Majesty rejoices over me and my fellow believers with joy and singing.

I pray LORD; remove sorrow and reproach that burden me.

Dear Heavenly Father, please grant me the grace to be 'on your side' and keep delighting You.

I thank You, Most High, in the name of Jesus Christ, Amen.

BIBLE PASSAGE
DANIEL 9: 16 – 17 & 19

16. LORD, according to all thy righteousness, I beseech thee, let thine anger and thy fury be turned away from thy city …: because for our sins, and for the iniquities of our fathers, … 17. Now therefore, O our God, hear the prayer of thy servant, and his supplications, and cause thy face to shine upon thy sanctuary that is desolate, for the Lord's sake. 19 O Lord, hear; O Lord, forgive; … thy people are called by thy name.

PRAYER

Most holy and Most High God, I regret most sorrowfully that we have gone astray from your guiding and blessed presence,

O LORD our God, Our world is sick and afflicted by self-inflicted maladies of greed, adultery, and idolatry, famine, wars, and plagues, because we have turned aside and away from your Word

Today Lord, I pray your Majesty, turn our hearts to Thee. Remove all stony hearts and replace them with flesh that abides in your words.

Please, Lord in mercy send your healing word and so heal our nation, indeed our world.

I pray in the name of Jesus Christ, our Lord, and Savior. Amen.

BIBLE PASSAGE
PSALM 150

1. Praise ye the **LORD. Praise God** in his sanctuary: praise him in the firmament of his power. **2. Praise** him for his mighty acts: praise him according to his excellent greatness. **3. Praise** him with the sound of the trumpet: praise him with the psaltery and harp. **4. Praise** him with the timbrel and dance: praise him with stringed instruments and organs. **5. Praise** him upon the loud cymbals: praise him upon the high-sounding cymbals. **6. Let** everything that hath breath praise the **LORD.** Praise ye the **LORD.**

The above Psalm **150: 1 - 6** is to be spoken, that vocalized, even chanted in an atmosphere of peace and joy.

The LORD God who promised to hear us before we call and answer us while we yet speak, Isaiah 65: 24, will meet you at the point of your need and beyond in Jesus' name.

CHAPTER 4

Pray According To God's Will

God's plan for believers, His Children is great, so affirms the Holy Scriptures in **Jeremiah 29: 11,** quoted below.

For I know the thoughts that I think toward you, saith the LORD, thoughts of peace, and not of evil, to give you an expected end.

We, believers, should gladly accept the above declaration of the Almighty God in faith and relate with Him as such when we pray. Secondly, our prayer must of necessity reflect God's will for us. The book of **James 4: 3** quoted below shows this to us

Ye ask, and receive not, because ye ask amiss, that ye may consume it upon your lusts.

God hears and grants all prayers of His children when they pray and ask according to his will. Get down to it; He is waiting for your Prayer.

BIBLE PASSAGE
PSALM 51: 1 - 4

1. Have mercy upon me, O God, according to thy loving kindness: according unto the multitude of thy tender mercies blot out my transgressions.2.Wash me thoroughly from mine iniquity, and cleanse me from my sin. 3. For I acknowledge my transgressions: and my sin is ever before me.4.Against thee, thee only, have I sinned, and done this evil in thy sight: that thou mightest be justified when thou speakest, and be clear when thou judgest.

PRAYER
Dear holy and merciful God, I'm ashamed that I have sinned against Your Majesty and my fellow brethren. I deeply regret and I'm sorry for all the sins I have committed in my thoughts, utterances, and actions as well as omissions. LODRD, I plead the precious and cleansing blood of my Savior Jesus Christ, shed for me and the unparallel sacrifice of His life on the cross at Cavalry. Father of mercies, a contrite heart you will not despise; please have mercy on me and forgive me. Father LORD, create a clean heart in me and renew a right spirit within me. Restore the joy of Your salvation to me O LORD and uphold me with Your free spirit. Amen.

BIBLE PASSAGE
PSALM 84: 8 - 11

8. O LORD God of hosts, hear my prayer: give ear, O God of Jacob. Selah. 9. Behold, O God our shield, and look upon the face of thine anointed. 10. For a day in thy courts is better than a thousand. I had rather be a doorkeeper in the house of my God, than to dwell in the tents of wickedness. 11. For the LORD God is a sun and shield: the LORD will give grace and glory: no good thing will he withhold from them that walk uprightly.

PRAYER

Father LORD, I come humbly unto your throne of Grace in the name my Lord Jesus Christ, Your only begotten Son.

I seek Your grace and glory to dwell in your presence always.

Father, LORD I also ask for anointing grace to walk uprightly consistently before Your Majesty all the days of my earthly life and reign with You hereafter.

O LORD God of hosts, attend to my prayer: and mercifully grant my requests which I prayed in the name Jesus Christ.

Amen.

BIBLE PASSAGE

DEUTERONOMY 28: 3 -6

3. Blessed shalt thou be in the city, and blessed shalt thou be in the field. 4. Blessed shall be the fruit of thy body, and the fruit of thy ground, and the fruit of thy cattle, the increase of thy kine, and the flocks of thy sheep. 5. Blessed shall be thy basket and thy store. 6. Blessed shalt thou be when thou comest in, and blessed shalt thou be when thou goest out.

PRAYER

King of kings and LORD of lords, I'm appreciative of your manifold blessings upon me, all of which I accept with faith.

I thank, adore, and worship your Excellency for blessing me in the city, in my work and business.

LORD, I bless and thank you for your all-round blessings upon me and all that is mine.

Father LORD accept my thanks and appreciation in the name of Jesus Christ, my Lord, and Savior.

Amen and Amen.

BIBLE PASSAGE
ESTHER 2: 16 - 18

16. So Esther was taken unto king Ahasuerus into his house royal in the tenth month, which is the month Tebeth, in the seventh year of his reign.17. And the king loved Esther above all the women, and she obtained grace and favour in his sight more than all the virgins; so that he set the royal crown upon her head, and made her queen instead of Vashti.18. Then the king made a great feast unto all his princes and his servants, even Esther's feast; and he made a release to the provinces, and gave gifts, according to the state of the king.

PRAYER

O LORD my God, who made Esther, a slave in her land of captivity to obtain grace, and favor in the sight of the king and to love her, mercifully attend to me needs.

I pray Your Excellency, LORD, in the name my Savior, Jesus Christ to grant me to obtain grace, and favor of people in my work and relationships.

Father, LORD, I thank Your Majesty in the name of my Savior Jesus Christ.

Amen.

BIBLE PASSAGE

PSALM 19: 1-3 & 13

1. The heavens declare the glory of God; and the firmament sheweth his handy work. 2. Day unto day uttereth speech, and night unto night sheweth knowledge. 3. There is no speech nor language, where their voice is not heard. 13. Keep back thy servant also from presumptuous sins; let them not have dominion over me: then shall I be upright, and I shall be innocent from the great transgression.

PRAYER

I thank you Father for your protection over me and all mine throughout the night. I'm grateful to you dear Heavenly Father for the gift of life, and excellent health on a new day,

Dear Lord, I need your protection, and victory over temptation, and sin; let them not have dominion over me but give me victory over them this day.

I pray that you grant me success in my endeavors this day.

I pray in the name of my Savior, Lord Jesus Christ. Amen.

BIBLE PASSAGE
ISAIAH 55: 10 - 12

10. For as the rain cometh down, and the snow from heaven, and returneth not thither, but watereth the earth, and maketh it bring forth and bud, that it may give seed to the sower, and bread to the eater: 11. So shall my word be that goeth forth out of my mouth: it shall not return unto me void, but it shall accomplish that which I please, and it shall prosper in the thing whereto I sent it. 12. For ye shall go out with joy, and be led forth with peace: the mountains and the hills shall break forth before you into singing, and all the trees of the field shall clap their hands.

PRAYER
O LORD, Thou whose word cannot fail but must always be fulfilled, mercifully let your word of favor, grace, and blessing be fulfilled this day in my life as you did in Esther's case.

Dear LORD, grant my request in Jesus' name,
Amen.

BIBLE PASSAGE
PSALM 32: 8 - 9

8. I will instruct thee and teach thee in the way which thou shalt go: I will guide thee with mine eye. 9. Be ye not as the horse, or as the mule, which have no understanding: whose mouth must be held in with bit and bridle, lest they come near unto thee.

PRAYER

Your mercy and love have preserved me to see this beautiful new day, Lord, I'm very grateful.

I seek your protection and guidance as you've promised that you will instruct and teach me in the way that I should go, even guide me with your blessed eyes.

I know that when you do all these for me, I shall be free from errors, overcome temptation, and sin.

Grant my request O Lord for I ask in the name of my Lord, and Savior, Jesus Christ.

Amen.

BIBLE PASSAGE
ISAIAH 54: 17
No weapon that is formed against thee shall prosper; and every tongue that shall rise against thee in judgment thou shalt condemn. This is the heritage of the servants of the LORD, and their righteousness is of me, saith the LORD

PRAYER
In your name Lord Jesus Christ, I come against errors, sickness, accident, and every malevolent spirit and obtain instant and permanent victory over them.
I obtain victory for I rely on your infallible word that no weapon formed against me shall prosper and that any tongue that rises against me in judgment shall be condemned, and stands condemned.
Thank you Almighty God, for I prayed in of my Lord and Savior, Jesus' name.
Amen

BIBLE PASSAGE
JAMES 4: 6 - 8
6. But he giveth more grace. Wherefore he saith, God resisteth the proud, but giveth grace unto the humble. 7. Submit yourselves therefore to God. Resist the devil, and he will flee from you. 8. Draw nigh to God, and he will draw nigh to you. Cleanse your hands, ye sinners; and purify your hearts, ye double-minded.

PRAYER
Dear heavenly Father, I come humbly again unto your Throne of Grace in the name of Jesus Christ.

I need your help, Lord, to overcome Satan and sin; for on my own I can do nothing about them.

I therefore humbly ask Your Majesty for grace to always humble myself before Your Majesty, depart from sin, cleanse my entire essence, and cleave unto Your Majesty.

Father Lord, please mercifully grant my requests for I ask in the name of Jesus Christ, Amen.

BIBLE PASSAGE
PSALM 118: 24 - 28

24. This is the day which the LORD hath made; we will rejoice and be glad in it. 25. Save now, I beseech thee, O LORD: O LORD, I beseech thee, send now prosperity. 26. Blessed be he that cometh in the name of the LORD: we have blessed you out of the house of the LORD. 27. God is the LORD, which hath shewed us light: bind the sacrifice with cords, even unto the horns of the altar. 28. Thou art my God, and I will praise thee: thou art my God, I will exalt thee.

PRAYER
Almighty and eternal God, I thank you for admitting me into your presence in the name of Jesus Christ my Savior. I appreciate your pleasant disposition to our prosperity.

Dear Lord, I pray you to send now prosperity unto me. Bless the work of my hands, Lord, for your goodness' sake.

Look mercifully upon me, my God, and prosper my endeavors this day.

Thank you Almighty God, for I prayed in the name that's above all names, Lord Jesus Christ,
Amen.

BIBLE PASSAGE

MATTHEW 11: 28 -30

28. Come unto me, all ye that labour and are heavy laden, and I will give you rest.29. Take my yoke upon you, and learn of me; for I am meek and lowly in heart: and ye shall find rest unto your souls.30.For my yoke is easy, and my burden is light.

PRAYER

O Lord Jesus Christ our Savior, I come in response to your kind call, when you said all who labor and are heavy-laden should come to you.

I come with my (educational/unemployment/financial/family/ health/ marital etc,) burden unto you.

Help me O Lord for I'm ready to take your yoke and burden and also learn of you.

Help resolve all the above burdens to my advantage today, Lord I pray.

I thank You, Lord for granting my requests, for I prayed in Your name Lord Jesus,
Amen.

BIBLE PASSAGE
MATTHEW 18: 18
18 Verily I say unto you, whatsoever ye shall bind on earth shall be bound in heaven: and whatsoever ye shall loose on earth shall be loosed in heaven.

PRAYER
Dear Lord Jesus Christ, my Savior,
I appreciate your love and the privilege and benefits of praying in your hallowed name.
In exercise of the power, I bind every contrary power, every malevolent spirit operating in and around my life.
As I bind you, evil ones, on earth in the name Jesus Christ, you are so bound in heaven.
In the name of Jesus Christ, I cast you all to burn in the fire of God, for the LORD our God is a consuming fire and you are consumed.
It is done in the name of Jesus Christ,
Amen, and Amen.

BIBLE PASSAGE
PSALM 118: 15 - 17
15. The voice of rejoicing and salvation is in the tabernacles of the righteous: the right hand of the LORD doeth valiantly. 16. The right hand of the LORD is exalted: the right hand of the LORD doeth valiantly.17. I shall not die, but live, and declare the works of the LORD.

PRAYER
Our dear Heavenly Father, in Jesus' miracles working name I come unto your throne of mercy for grace to live and not die.
I affirm and confess, in the name Jesus Christ, your only begotten Son, my Lord, and Savior that I shall not die but live and declare your works, dear LORD.
Similarly, my family members shall not die; they too shall live to declare the work of God.
I thank you Almighty God for granting my request, for I prayed in the name of Jesus Christ.
Amen.

,

BIBLE PASSAGE
PSALM 35: 27 - 28

27. Let them shout for joy, and be glad, that favour my righteous cause: yea, let them say continually, let the LORD be magnified, which hath pleasure in the prosperity of his servant. 28. And my tongue shall speak of thy righteousness and of thy praise all the day long.

PRAYER
Almighty and eternal God, I come humbly into your presence in the name of my Savior Jesus Christ.
I'm gratefully delighted for your kindness and pleasure in my prosperity.
Dear Lord, let your name be magnified in my life even as you prosper my endeavors this day and henceforth O Lord, for your goodness sake.
Almighty God, thank you for granting my request which I made in the name that's above all names, Lord Jesus Christ.
Amen.

BIBLE PASSAGE
EPHESIANS 1: 3 - 4
3. Blessed be the God and Father of our Lord Jesus Christ, who hath blessed us with all spiritual blessings in heavenly places in Christ: 4. According as he hath chosen us in him before the foundation of the world, that we should be holy and without blame before him in love:

PRAYER
My dear Heavenly Father, I'm elated by your word blessing us your children.
I now come in faith, requesting that you mercifully manifest your blessing upon me and all mine.
Father, LORD, I plead in the hallowed name of your only begotten Son, Jesus Christ that you manifest all the spiritual blessings in heavenly places in Christ in my life.
Father LORD, I thank you for granting my request which I have made in the name of my Lord Jesus Christ.
Amen.

BIBLE PASSAGE
EPHESIANS 2: 8 - 10
8. For by grace are ye saved through faith; and that not of yourselves: it is the gift of God: 9. Not of works, lest any man should boast. 10. For we are his workmanship, created in Christ Jesus unto good works, which God hath before ordained that we should walk in them.

PRAYER
Dear LORD, I appreciate your saving me by grace and not for any good I've done.
I also appreciate that I'm your workmanship, created in Christ Jesus unto good works. Now LORD please grant that I immediately begin to live displaying the good works I'm created in Christ Jesus for.
I'm thankful LORD for granting my request, which I brought to you in the name of Jesus Christ.
Amen.

BIBLE PASSAGE

PSALM 86: 1 - 7

1. Bow down thine ear, O LORD, hear me: for I am poor and needy. 2. Preserve my soul; for I am holy: O thou my God, save thy servant that trusteth in thee. 3. Be merciful unto me, O Lord: for I cry unto thee daily. 4. Rejoice the soul of thy servant: for unto thee, O Lord, do I lift up my soul. 5. For thou, Lord, art good, and ready to forgive; and plenteous in mercy unto all them that call upon thee. 6. Give ear, O LORD, unto my prayer; and attend to the voice of my supplications. 7. In the day of my trouble I will call upon thee: for thou wilt answer me.

PRAYER

I come to you, in the name of Jesus Christ O LORD God who knows and can do all things.

I'm here in your presence with my care and burden because I trust you'll hear and deliver me from all my troubles. I need your intervention in my life, particularly in my finances. Unto you, you alone in whom I trust do I cry and present my petition to, O LORD.

Rejoice and gladden my heart by lifting and prospering me today and henceforth, O LORD.

I thank you, LORD for granting my requests, Amen.

BIBLE PASSAGE
PSALM 107: 20 - 22

20. He sent his word, and healed them, and delivered them from their destructions. 21. Oh that men would praise the LORD for his goodness, and for his wonderful works to the children of men! 22. And let them sacrifice the sacrifices of thanksgiving, and declare his works with rejoicing.

PRAYER

I appreciate you, thou Most High whose words heal.

I regret most sorrowfully that we have gone astray from your guiding and blessed words and presence.

O LORD our God, Our world is sick and afflicted by self-inflicted maladies of greed, adultery, and idolatry, famine, wars, and plagues, because we have turned aside and away from your Word.

Today Lord, I pray your Majesty, turn our hearts to Thee.

Remove all stony hearts, and replace them with flesh that abides in your words.

Please, Lord in mercy send your healing word, and so heal our nation, indeed our world.

I pray in the name of Jesus Christ, our Lord, and Savior. Amen.

BIBLE PASSAGE

ISAIAH 53: 3 - 5

3. He is despised and rejected of men; a man of sorrows, and acquainted with grief: and we hid as it were our faces from him; he was despised, and we esteemed him not.4. Surely he hath borne our griefs, and carried our sorrows: yet we did esteem him stricken, smitten of God, and afflicted. 5. But he was wounded for our transgressions, he was bruised for our iniquities: the chastisement of our peace was upon him; and with his stripes we are healed.

PRAYER

Dear great healer, Lord Jesus Christ I come humbly to possess my healing which you perfected long before my mother conceived me in her womb.

Thou Lamb of God who shed your precious blood for my redemption and salvation, even salvation from sickness or any affliction, I possess my healing NOW in your name Lord Jesus Christ.

I'm grateful to you my Lord and Savior Jesus Christ for healing me.

Amen.

CHAPTER 5

Claim God's Infallible Promises

The loss of Paradise means that the benevolences of God are no longer automatically available to mankind. Note that quite a lot of His benevolences are still available to all. However, the special ones are faith-based. The nine supernatural gifts of the Holy Ghost (**1 Corinthians 12: 4-10**) are examples of those benevolences that can only be bestowed and received through faith in God.

However, because of God's immense love for mankind, He has given all mankind his only begotten Son, so that man should not perish but regain eternal life. Of course, God gives a condition, which is that this redemption and restoration promise is available ONLY to those who believe in him.

For God so loved the world, that he gave his only begotten Son, that whosoever believeth in him should not perish, but have everlasting life.
John 3: 16

The Following are some of the promises made by God, who cannot lie (**Titus 1: 2**) but is faithful (**Hebrews 10: 23**), to believers. These promises are certain, sure, and accessible by faith in God through His Son Jesus Christ.

Trust & Confidence In God

For God so loved the world, that he gave his only begotten Son, that whosoever believeth in him should not perish, but have everlasting life.
John 3: 16

For we are saved by hope: but hope that is seen is not hope: for what a man seeth, why doth he yet hope for?
Romans 8: 24

And we know that all things work together for good to them that love God, to them who are the called according to his purpose.
Romans 8: 28

Likewise the Spirit also helpeth our infirmities: for we know not what we should pray for as we ought: but the Spirit itself maketh intercession for us with groanings which cannot be uttered. **Romans 8: 26**

As many as received him, to them gave he power to become the sons of God, even to them that believe on his name:
John 1: 12

Some trust in chariots, and some in horses: but we will remember the name of the LORD our God. They are brought down and fallen: but we are risen, and stand upright.
Psalm 20: 7 & 8

 The LORD is my light and my salvation; whom shall I fear? the LORD is the strength of my life; of whom shall I be afraid? When the wicked, even mine enemies and my foes, came upon me to eat up my flesh, they stumbled and fell.
Psalm 27: 1 & 2

I will extol thee, O LORD; for thou hast lifted me up, and hast not made my foes to rejoice over me. O LORD my God, I cried unto thee, and thou hast healed me.
Psalm 30: 19 & 20

Trust in the LORD, and do good; so shalt thou dwell in the land, and verily thou shalt be fed. Delight thyself also in the LORD: and he shall give

thee the desires of thine heart. Commit thy way unto
the LORD; trust also in him; and he shall bring it to
pass.
Psalm 37: 3 – 5

And the spirit of the LORD shall rest upon him, the
spirit of wisdom and understanding, the spirit of
counsel and might, the spirit of knowledge and of
the fear of the LORD;
Isaiah 11: 2

Thus saith the LORD to his anointed, to Cyrus,
whose right hand I have holden, to subdue nations
before him; and I will lose the loins of kings, to open
before him the two leaved gates; and the gates shall
not be shut; I will go before thee, and make the
crooked places straight: I will break in pieces the
gates of brass, and cut in sunder the bars of iron:
And I will give thee the treasures of darkness, and
hidden riches of secret places, that thou mayest
know that I, the LORD, which call thee by thy
name, am the God of Israel.
Isaiah 45: 1 - 3

Thus saith the Lord GOD, Behold, I will lift up
mine hand to the Gentiles, and set up my standard
to the people: and they shall bring thy sons in their

arms, and thy daughters shall be carried upon their shoulders. And kings shall be thy nursing fathers, and their queens thy nursing mothers: they shall bow down to thee with their face toward the earth, and lick up the dust of thy feet; and thou shalt know that I am the LORD: for they shall not be ashamed that wait for me.
Isaiah 49: 22 - 23

24. Shall the prey be taken from the mighty, or the lawful captive delivered? 25. But thus saith the LORD, Even the captives of the mighty shall be taken away, and the prey of the terrible shall be delivered: for I will contend with him that contendeth with thee, and I will save thy children. 26. And I will feed them that oppress thee with their own flesh; and they shall be drunken with their own blood, as with sweet wine: and all flesh shall know that I the LORD am thy Saviour and thy Redeemer, the mighty One of Jacob.
Isaiah 49: 24 - 26

Defense & Protection against Enemies:

No weapon that is formed against thee shall prosper; and every tongue that shall rise against thee in

judgment thou shalt condemn. This is the heritage of the servants of the LORD, and their righteousness is of me, saith the LORD.
Isaiah 54: 17

For the Lord GOD will help me; therefore shall I not be confounded: therefore have I set my face like a flint, and I know that I shall not be ashamed. He is near that justifieth me; who will contend with me? let us stand together: who is mine adversary? let him come near to me. Behold, the Lord GOD will help me; who is he that shall condemn me? lo, they all shall wax old as a garment; the moth shall eat them up.
Isaiah 50: 7 - 9

Shall the prey be taken from the mighty, or the lawful captive delivered? But thus saith the LORD, Even the captives of the mighty shall be taken away, and the prey of the terrible shall be delivered: for I will contend with him that contendeth with thee, and I will save thy children. And I will feed them that oppress thee with their own flesh; and they shall be drunken with their own blood, as with sweet wine: and all flesh shall know that I the LORD am thy Saviour and thy Redeemer, the mighty One of Jacob.
Isaiah 49: 24 - 26

Take counsel together, and it shall come to nought; speak the word, and it shall not stand: for God is with us.
Isaiah 8: 10

Behold, I and the children whom the LORD hath given me are for signs and for wonders in Israel from the LORD of hosts, which dwelleth in mount Zion.
Isaiah 8: 18

Protection And Provision:

When the enemy shall come in like a flood, the Spirit of the LORD shall lift up a standard against him.
Isaiah 59: 19

Now the Egyptians are men, and not God; and their horses flesh, and not spirit. When the LORD shall stretch out his hand, both he that helpeth shall fall, and he that is holpen shall fall down, and they all shall fail together.
Isaiah 31: 3

Wherefore thus saith the LORD God of hosts, Because ye speak this word, behold, I will make my

words in thy mouth fire, and this people wood, and
it shall devour them.
Jeremiah 5: 14

 And it shall come to pass in that day, that his
burden shall be taken away from off thy shoulder,
and his yoke from off thy neck, and the yoke shall be
destroyed because of the anointing.
Isaiah 10: 27

<u>Prosperity</u>

3. Blessed shalt thou be in the city, and blessed shalt
thou be in the field. 4. Blessed shall be the fruit of
thy body, and the fruit of thy ground, and the fruit
of thy cattle, the increase of thy kine, and the flocks
of thy sheep. 5. Blessed shall be thy basket and thy
store. 6. Blessed shalt thou be when thou comest in,
and blessed shalt thou be when thou goest out.
Deuteronomy 28: 3 - 4

27. And he came near, and kissed him: and he
smelled the smell of his raiment, and blessed him,
and said, See, the smell of my son is as the smell of a
field which the LORD hath blessed: 28. Therefore
God give thee of the dew of heaven, and the fatness

of the earth, and plenty of corn and wine: 29. Let people serve thee, and nations bow down to thee: be lord over thy brethren, and let thy mother's sons bow down to thee: cursed be every one that curseth thee, and blessed be he that blesseth thee.
Genesis 27: 27 - 29

25.Even by the God of thy father, who shall help thee; and by the Almighty, who shall bless thee with blessings of heaven above, blessings of the deep that lieth under, blessings of the breasts, and of the womb: 26. The blessings of thy father have prevailed above the blessings of my progenitors unto the utmost bound of the everlasting hills: they shall be on the head of Joseph, and on the crown of the head of him that was separate from his brethren.
Genesis 48: 25 - 26

The LORD is my shepherd; I shall not want. He maketh me to lie down in green pastures: he leadeth me beside the still waters. He restoreth my soul: he leadeth me in the paths of righteousness for his name's sake. Yea, though I walk through the valley of the shadow of death, I will fear no evil: for thou art with me; thy rod and thy staff they comfort me. Thou preparest a table before me in the presence of mine enemies: thou anointest my head with oil; my

cup runneth over. Surely goodness and mercy shall
follow me all the days of my life: and I will dwell in
the house of the LORD forever.
Psalm 23: 1 – 6

But my God shall supply all your need according to
his riches in glory by Christ Jesus.
Philippians 4: 19

Surely goodness and mercy shall follow me all the
days of my life: and I will dwell in the house of the
LORD forever.
Psalm23: 6

I will say of the LORD, He is my refuge and my
fortress: my God; in him will I trust. Surely he shall
deliver thee from the snare of the fowler, and from
the noisome pestilence.
Psalm 91: 2 - 3

Healing & General Wellbeing

There shall nothing cast their young, nor be barren,
in thy land: the number of thy days I will fulfill.
Exodus 23: 26

For I will restore health unto thee, and I will heal thee of thy wounds, saith the LORD; because they called thee an Outcast, saying, This is Zion, whom no man seeketh after.
Jeremiah 30: 17

And ye shall serve the LORD your God, and he shall bless thy bread, and thy water; and I will take sickness away from the midst of thee.
Exodus 3: 25

But unto you that fear my name shall the Sun of righteousness arise with healing in his wings; and ye shall go forth, and grow up as calves of the stall.
Malachi 4: 2

Behold, I will bring it health and cure, and I will cure them, and will reveal unto them the abundance of peace and truth.
Jeremiah 33: 6

And the LORD will take away from thee all sickness, and will put none of the evil diseases of Egypt, which thou knowest, upon thee; but will lay them upon all them that hate thee.
Deuteronomy 7: 15

<u>**Over All Protection:**</u>

24. The LORD bless thee, and keep thee: 25. The LORD make his face shine upon thee, and be gracious unto thee: 26. The LORD lift up his countenance upon thee, and give thee peace. 27. And they shall put my name upon the children of Israel, and I will bless them.
Numbers 6: 24

1. The LORD is my light and my salvation; whom shall I fear? the LORD is the strength of my life; of whom shall I be afraid? 2. When the wicked, even mine enemies and my foes, came upon me to eat up my flesh, they stumbled and fell. 4. One thing have I desired of the LORD, that will I seek after; that I may dwell in the house of the LORD all the days of my life, to behold the beauty of the LORD, and to enquire in his temple. 5. For in the time of trouble he shall hide me in his pavilion: in the secret of his tabernacle shall he hide me; he shall set me up upon a rock.
Psalm27: 1 - 2, 4 - 5

With him is an arm of flesh; but with us is the LORD our God to help us, and to fight our battles.

And the people rested themselves upon the words of
Hezekiah king of Judah.
2 Chronicles 32: 8

Ye are of God, little children, and have overcome
them: because greater is he that is in you, than he
that is in the world.
1 John 4: 4

And five of you shall chase an hundred, and an
hundred of you shall put ten thousand to flight: and
your enemies shall fall before you by the sword.
Leviticus 26: 8

Books by Anthony Obasola **SHODERU**

Other works of Anthony Obasola Shoderu include: ANTICHRIST At The Doorstep?, POLITICS, SURVIVED To Thrive. Politics, Our Own, MY PSALTER, The Kingdom Call, You Too Can Do Exploits, Guarding The Home-Front, Looking Forward And God-Ward, The Vital Change You Need Now, Beheading Goliath With Goliath's Sword, Prosperity Is My Birthright, ENTER THE ANTI-CHRIST - The Last Days (Eschatology) Simplified, DON'T BE AFRAID, Overcome Your Fears Today, SUBMISSION In Marriage, MAN AND THE HOLY SPIRIT and 468 STRIPES FROM39 LASHES.